# ADVENTURES IN OPERATIONS MANAGEMENT

**Version 1.0**

**Automated Homework System**

D0145745

## Quant Systems
Charleston, SC

ISBN  0-918091-09-8

# Table of Contents

## Technical Skill Builder Summaries

# An Overview of the *Adventures* Concept

*Adventures in Operations Management* is a tutoring system designed to enhance the understanding of operations management concepts, improve problem solving skills, and make the process of learning more enjoyable. The *Adventures* system is designed to enhance motivation by providing tutoring to the student when it is requested, and enabling the student to test him/herself in a "fear free" environment. *Adventures* relies on the mastery level learning concept. That is, the student may take a test (certification) as many times as is necessary to demonstrate mastery of the material. There is no penalty for failing during the learning process--after all, failure is an important part of learning. We would like to think that the only way to "fail" any module is to quit trying.

Typically, instructors assign *Adventures in Operations Management* modules as they would assign homework from a book. Each module tutors and tests students on a concept in operations management. The problems that students solve are unique to each student, since problem scenarios, parameters, and key wording are randomly generated.

Students go to the school's computer lab or use their own computers to do the *Adventures* problem solving exercises. Each *Adventures* module begins in the learning mode where students work with our intelligent tutor. After developing confidence in their ability to solve problems, students will switch to the certification mode (testing) and attempt to demonstrate mastery of the topic. If they pass the module, a certification code is automatically logged and time-stamped into our database, the Classroom Management System. Students who are working at home can bring the certification code to the school's network and register it into the database. These codes are unique to each student and each module, and can be used to ensure that the problem solving exercises were completed. If a student does not pass the test, he/she can retake the test until mastery of the topic is demonstrated and the code is received.

3

# Installation Instructions for
# *Adventures in Operations Management*

If you have any questions or if we can be of assistance in any way, please don't hesitate to call us at (803) 571-2825.

## Minimum System Requirements

1. MS DOS 5.0 or higher
2. Windows 3.1 or higher
3. 15 MB of hard disk space

## Installation Procedure

1. If you have previously installed *Adventures in Operations Management*, delete the *Adventures in Ops. Mgmt.* program group as follows:

a. Click on the *Adventures in Ops. Mgmt.* icon once. The program group is properly selected if there is a box around the title of the group as shown below. (Note: The program group should <u>not</u> be open.)

b. Delete the program group by selecting **File** (Alt + F) and then **Delete** (Alt + D).

c. Confirm that you would like to delete the *Adventures in Ops. Mgmt.* program group by selecting **Yes** (Alt + Y).

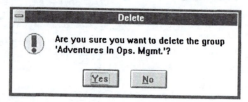

2. Install the new version of *Adventures in Ops. Mgmt.* as follows:

a. Insert the diskette labeled "*Adventures in Ops. Mgmt. Setup Disk #1*" in the floppy drive and then run MS Windows (if you are not already in Windows).

b. Select **File** (Alt + F) from the Program Manager main menu and then select **Run** (Alt + R) from the pull-down menu.

c. Type the path to the floppy drive in which you inserted the installation diskette and then type **setup**. For example, if you inserted the setup diskette into drive **a:** , type the following:

d. Press <Enter> or click on the **OK** button.

5

3. During the setup process you will be asked to do the following:

a. Type your name and your institution's name. Then select **Continue Setup**.

b. Confirm your input and then select **Continue Setup**.

c. Enter the path to the directory and the name of the directory in which you would like to install *Adventures in Operations Management*, and then select **Continue Setup**. In the following example, *Adventures in Operations Management* will be stored in the AIOM directory on the hard drive **c:**. (Note: The default is c:\AIOM.)

d. After selecting **Continue Setup** in part (c) , a box will appear displaying the progress of the setup. If you would like to quit the setup program at any time, select **Exit Setup**.

e. During the setup process, you will be prompted to insert more disks. Insert the disks, in the order that they are requested, into the same drive that you inserted Setup Disk #1. Select **OK** after each disk is inserted.

f. Type the name that you would like to call the *Adventures* program group in the box below and then click on the **OK** button. (Note: The default is *Adventures in Ops. Mgmt.*)

g. The setup program will create a program group called *Adventures in Ops. Mgmt.* (or the name you entered).

Note 1: Windows creates the group file name aiom<u>name</u>.grp for the group, where name=the first 4 characters of the name given to the program group.

Note 2: The installation procedure is the same whether you are installing the program onto an individual computer or onto a network. However, for network installations, if the individual workstations do not access Windows from the network drive, the program group will have to be set up on each individual workstation.

7

# Starting *Adventures in Operations Management*

1. Run Microsoft Windows.

2. Open the *Adventures in Operations Management* program group by double-clicking on the *Adventures in Ops. Mgmt.* icon.

3. The *Adventures in Ops. Mgmt.* program group will appear. To start *Adventures in Operations Management*, double-click on the *AIOM Index* icon.

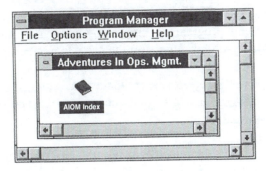

8

4. The *Adventures in Operations Management* menu will appear.

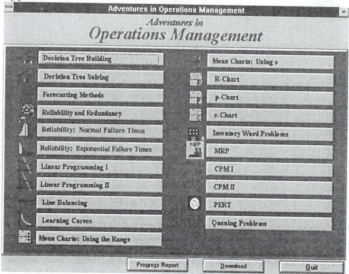

a. To see a report of your progress or to register your certification code, select **Progress Report** (Alt + P).

b. To download *Adventures in Operations Management* from the network, select **Download** (Alt + D) .

c. If you wish to exit the *Adventures in Operations Management* menu, select **Quit** (Alt + Q).

### 5. Selecting a Module

From the *Adventures in Operations Management* menu, click one time on a module name button. (Or press Alt + the underlined letter.)

6. After a module is selected, the title screen for that module will appear.

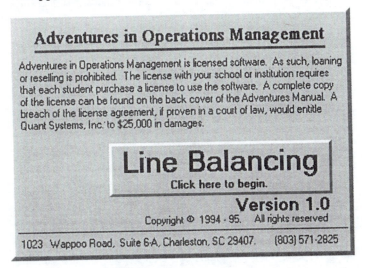

Click one time on the module name button. The authorization code entry box will appear.

### 7. The Authorization Code

Students will receive personal authorization codes from their instructor once they have completed and turned in the coupons that are attached to their manuals. The authorization code is a 30 digit alphanumeric code that is an encryption of a student's name. The code is used by the *Adventures* system to identify students as they are working on the *Adventures in Operations Management* modules.

The program will request an authorization code each time a module is opened. Students may either type in the code by hand, load it from a disk, or load it from a drive on a computer. If the code has not already been saved on a disk or in a file on a computer, then the code must be typed in at least one time.

## Typing in Your Code

Type each 6 digit section of your code in the spaces provided in the code entry box. After typing in a section of the code, move to the next section by pressing <Enter>. After typing in the last section of the code, either press <Enter> or click on the **OK** button.

**Enter your authorization code:**

Ok    Cancel

<F1> - Load from disk

**Cautions:**

1) Make sure to type the **letter I** (as in igloo) when your code contains this letter. Authorization codes do not contain the **letter L** or the **number 1**.

2) Make sure to press **<Enter>** after each section of code. Your code may not work if you press **<Tab>** instead.

## Saving Your Code

After you type in your code and it is accepted, the program will ask you if you want to save your code to a disk. You can save your code on a floppy disk or on your computer.

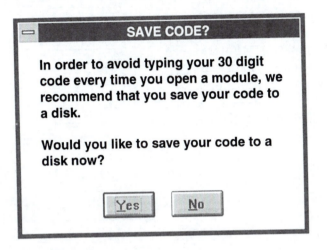

If you do not want to save your code now, select **No**. You will have to type in your code every time you open a module until you save your code.

If you select **Yes**, the program will ask you to choose the drive and directory on which you wish to save your code.

In this example, the code is being saved to a file named
**access.cod** that is in the **root directory** of a floppy disk in
**drive a:**. After you choose the drive and directory, click on
the **OK** button or press <Enter>.

**Loading Your Previously Saved Code**

When the code entry box
appears, press the <F1>
key or click on the **Load
From Disk** button.

From the Open box, choose the drive and directory where your
code is located. Then either double click on the access.cod
file name, click on the **OK** button, or press <Enter>.

8. When your code has been accepted, the following box will appear:

Select **Yes** to continue.

9. Next, you will be asked to select the Series # that was assigned by your instructor.

Choose a Series # and then select **OK**. You can now proceed with the module.

Note: If your instructor is using CMS and you are working on the school's network, the series is set by your instructor and you will not be prompted to select a series code.

# Modes of Operation

Some of the *Adventures in Operations Management* modules have a Demonstration Mode and some have a Help Option. Every module has a Practice Mode and a Certification Mode.

**Demonstration Mode**

The Demonstration Mode highlights the module's unique features by walking the student through a sample problem. The step by step instructions were created so that instructors will not have to spend class time showing students how to navigate each module.

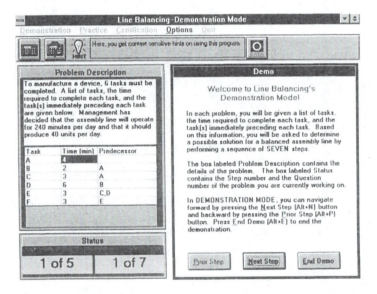

The Demonstration Mode features the following information:

1. the type of problems that students will be expected to solve,

2. the mechanics of using the module's unique features, and

3. the criteria for mastery.

## Help Option

The Help Option provides information on the basic modes of operation as well as any unique features which the module might have.

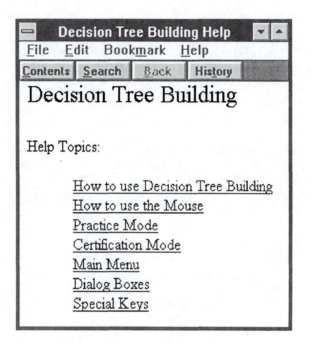

## Practice Mode

In Practice Mode, help is provided through the **Tutor**, **Help**, or **Hint** buttons. The **Tutor** button gives a discussion of the topic, detailed examples, and a detailed solution to each randomly generated problem. The **Help** button gives a description of the mechanics of entering an answer or using the tools.

The **Hint** button asks questions and gives formulas that help students answer the questions.

17

## Certification Mode

The Certification Mode is a testing mode in which the **Tutor** and **Hint** buttons are removed. In this mode, students must correctly answer 80% to 90% of the questions in order to certify. The percentage required to certify varies by module. If students are unsuccessful in their first attempt to certify, they may try again as many times as is necessary to master the concept.

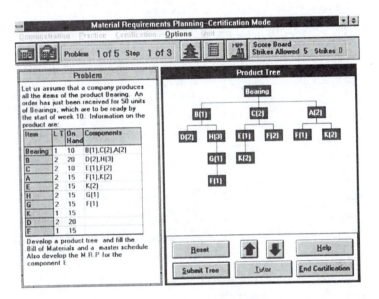

Once students successfully complete a module, the program produces a five or six digit certification code that is unique to each student and to each module. Students may want to record this code in the Record Book that is in the back of their manual.

Since the certification code is not known in advance by students, it serves as a reliable measure of successful homework completion. The certification code is either submitted physically to the instructor or electronically through the Classroom Management System.

# Commands and Conventions

In documenting the *Adventures* software, we use angle brackets <> to enclose a key that is to be depressed. Do <u>not</u> type the angle brackets.

## Scrolling

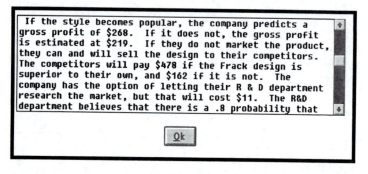

Some problems cannot be viewed completely at one time. Therefore, you will need to scroll down by either clicking on the down arrow in the scroll box, or by holding down the <Ctrl> key and pressing the <↓> key.

## Selecting an Option or a Button

If you wish to select an option (or a button), click the mouse on the option (or the button), or hold down the <Alt> key and press the key of the underlined letter at the same time.

<u>Example</u>: To select the **Practice** option on the horizontal menu bar, click the mouse on the word **Practice,** or hold down the <Alt> key and press <P> at the same time.

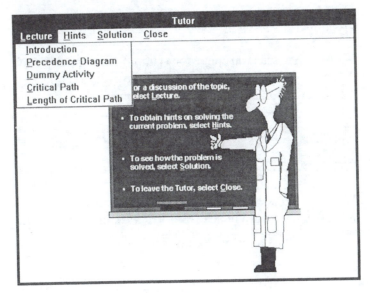

## The Tutor Button

The **Tutor** button is only available in the Practice Mode of some modules. The **Tutor** gives access to the **Lecture**, **Hints**, and **Solution** options.

The Lecture is designed to help students understand the concepts of the module. It also gives example problems with detailed solutions. To open the Lecture, select **Lecture** from the Tutor screen and choose a page from the pull-down menu.

Move through the Lecture by selecting the **Next Page/Previous Page** buttons, or go directly to a page by selecting **Lecture** and choosing the desired page from the pull-down menu.

If the **Solution** option is selected from the Tutor screen or from one of the Lecture screens, students will be shown in detail how to solve the given problem and then they must go on to the next problem.

If the **Hints** option is selected from the Tutor screen or from one of the Lecture screens, students will be shown small steps that will gradually lead them toward the solution of the given problem.

Adventures in Operations Management

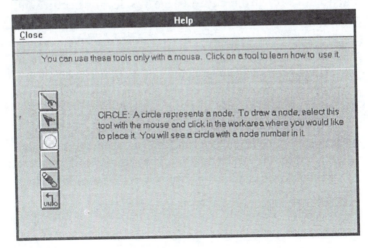

## The Help Button

When necessary, a **Help** button is available that gives detailed explanations of how an answer should be entered. It also gives directions on how to use the tool buttons available in the module.

22

## The Toolbar

Several modules have a toolbar available under the horizontal menu bar. Two tools that will be on most toolbars are the Calculator and the Calculator Help. If a tool has a related help tool, it will be located directly to the right of the tool and have a red question mark on it.

Other tools that can be found on the tool bar will depend on the module. For example, the tool bar in the **Learning Curves** module has a tool that displays a learning curve table for the given problem and a help tool that explains the table. There is also a tool that displays a learning curve graph for the given problem.

The tools on the tool bar can be accessed by clicking on the tool buttons with the mouse. They can also be accessed from the **Options** pull-down menu.

# Classroom Management System (CMS)

The Classroom Management System is a database that allows students to enter their certification codes into the instructor's grade book. The system also allows students to view their personal progress reports and the instructor's syllabus.

### Enrolling in CMS

If CMS has been installed, students entering an *Adventures* module or the Student Report Program for the first time will be prompted to enroll in CMS.

First, they will be asked to select their professor and enroll in the appropriate section.

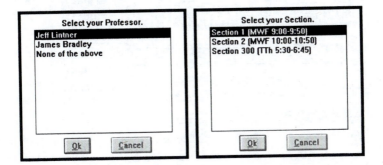

Once the selections have been made, the students will be prompted to confirm their selections.

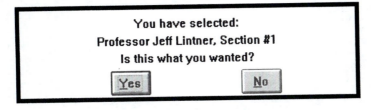

The student's selections will be acknowledged with the following box.

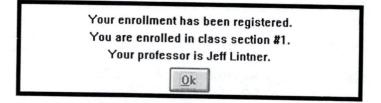

> Your enrollment has been registered.
> You are enrolled in class section #1.
> Your professor is Jeff Lintner.
>
> [ Ok ]

After the students have enrolled in an instructor's section, they will not be prompted to enroll again.

## The Student Report Program

During the installation of CMS, a button called "Progress Report" will be added to the *Adventures in Operations Management* Index menu. Students will use this program to enter their certification codes and review their progress.

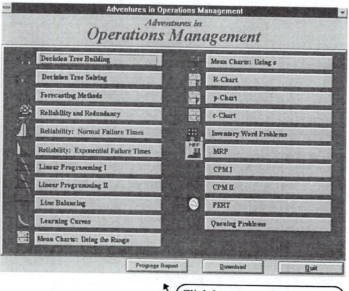

Click here to register certificates and view progress.

25

## Registering a Certificate

Once students have certified in a module, they can register their certificates in the instructor's grade book by performing the following steps.

a. Select **Progress Report** from the AIOM Index menu.
b. Enter the access code.
c. Select: **Register, Register Certificates**.

d. Select the appropriate module and then select: **Register**.

e. Enter the certification code for the module and then select: **OK**.

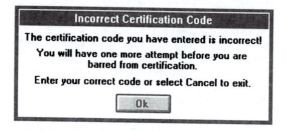

f. If students enter the correct certification code for the module, they will be notified that the certification has been registered.

Note: If an invalid code is entered, students will be notified that the code is invalid.

**Incorrect Certification Code**

The certification code you have entered is incorrect!
You will have one more attempt before you are barred from certification.
Enter your correct code or select Cancel to exit.

Ok

If an invalid certification code is entered twice, students will be barred from certifying in the module.

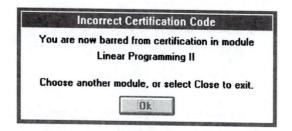

27

## Viewing a Progress Report or the Instructor's Syllabus

### Viewing a Progress Report

Students may view a report of their progress to date by selecting the **Progress Report** button from the AIOM Index menu. The progress report will be displayed automatically.

If the report does not all fit on one page, the students can click on the arrows of the scroll bar to move the report up or down.

```
┌──────────────────────────────────────────────────────────────┐
│ ▭                    Progress Report                    ▼  ▲  │
├──────────────────────────────────────────────────────────────┤
│ File   Register                                             ↕ │
│                                                                │
│                       Student Name : TEST F                    │
│           Access Code : 7XH2Y3J642W6WXWUY2KZRJI4HD6EXV         │
│                                                                │
│                   Key to Certification Codes                   │
│          Code             Meaning                              │
│          ────             ───────                              │
│          (T)              Certificate turned in on time        │
│          (L)              Certificate turned in late           │
│                                                                │
│                                                                │
│                   Key to Other Fields                          │
│          Code             Meaning                              │
│          ────             ───────                              │
│          Test 1           Test to see if program screws up     │
│                                                                │
│                          Certificates                          │
│                          ────────────                          │
│ LINEAR PROG 1 : 04/11/95 (T)      LINEAR PROG 2  : Barred      │
│ DEC TREE BUILD: Due 08/11/95      DEC TREE SOLVE : Due 08/11/95│
│ INVENT DROP   : Due 08/16/95      QUEUEING DROP  : Due 08/16/95│
└──────────────────────────────────────────────────────────────┘
```

### Viewing the Instructor's Syllabus

If the instructor has placed his or her syllabus in the CMS database, students may view the instructor's syllabus by selecting

### File, Display, Syllabus.

If the instructor has not placed his or her syllabus in the CMS database, the Syllabus selection will be disabled (gray).

```
┌──────────────────────────────────────────────────────────────┐
│ ─                        Syllabus                        ▼ ▲  │
│  ┌──────┐ Register                                            │
│  │ File │                                                     │
│ ┌─────────┬──────────────┐                                    │
│ │ Display │  Report       │ Production/Operations Management ↑│
│ │ Save    │ ◄ Syllabus    │ James Bradley                     │
│ │ Print Setup │          │                                    │
│ │ Print   │              │                                    │
│ │ Exit    │  ete the following modules by the due dates listed below │
│ └─────────┘ Any module which is turned in late will be subject to a 20% penalty. │
│                                                                │
│  Module Name                      Due Date                     │
│  Linear Programming I             5/25/95                      │
│  Linear Programming II            5/27/95                      │
│  Decision Tree Building           6/01/95                      │
│  Decision Tree Solving            6/02/95                      │
│  Inventory Problems               6/07/95                      │
│  Queuing Problems                 6/10/95                      │
│  Forecasting Methods              6/12/95                      │
│  Line Balancing                   6/15/95                      │
│  Learning Curves                  6/18/95                      │
│  Material Requirements Planning   6/20/95                      │
│                                                                │
│  The Adventures in Operations Management modules will account for 25% of your │
│  final grade.                                              ▼  │
└──────────────────────────────────────────────────────────────┘
```

If students would like to view their progress report after viewing the syllabus, they must select: **File**, **Display**, **Report**.

## Printing or Saving a Progress Report or the Syllabus

While viewing a progress report or the instructor's syllabus, students can print the report or the syllabus by selecting: **File**, **Print**, or they can save it by selecting: **File**, **Save**.

```
┌──────────────────────────────────────────────────────────────┐
│ ─                        Syllabus                        ▼ ▲  │
│  ┌──────┐ Register                                            │
│  │ File │                                                     │
│ ┌─────────────┐ Course:    Production/Operations Management ↑│
│ │ Display   ► │ Professor: James Bradley                     │
│ │ Save        │                                              │
│ │ Print Setup │                                              │
│ │             │                                              │
│ │ Exit        │ ete the following modules by the due dates listed below │
│ └─────────────┘ Any module which is turned in late will be subject to a 20% penalty │
│                                                                │
│  Module Name                      Due Date                     │
│  Linear Programming I             5/25/95                      │
│  Linear Programming II            5/27/95                      │
│  Decision Tree Building           6/01/95                      │
│  Decision Tree Solving            6/02/95                      │
└──────────────────────────────────────────────────────────────┘
```

# Decision Tree Building

This tutorial is designed to help you develop and refine skills in building decision tree models. A decision tree, shown below, is a graphical depiction of the alternatives available to a decision maker and the possible consequences of each alternative.

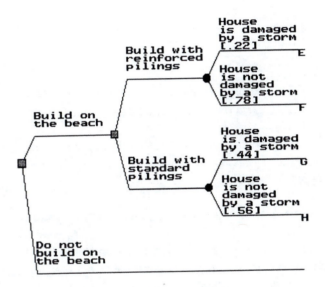

## To Begin

Select **Help** from the main menu and read each of the topics.

## Practice Mode

Go to the main menu and select **Practice**.

The following screen will appear:

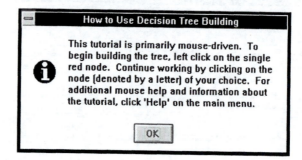

Select **OK** to continue.

## Step 1      Viewing the Problem

A box will appear with the problem inside. You may need to scroll to view the entire problem. While viewing the problem, you should take notes on the parameters of the problem and construct the appropriate decision tree. When you are finished viewing the problem, select **Ok**.

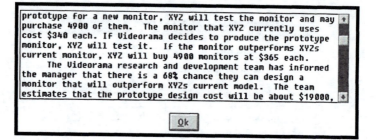

## Step 2      Drawing the Decision Tree

### SECTION 1

The first step in the drawing process is to click on the red node with your mouse.

■ ←———— **Start by left-clicking on this node.**

31

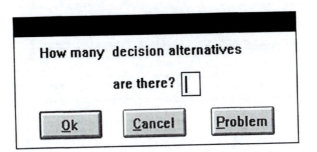

At this point you have three options:

1. place the number of decisions as defined in the problem into the box and select **Ok**,

2. select **Problem** to see the problem again,

3. select **Cancel** to return you to the previous screen.

After the number of decisions has been entered, you will be given a screen that permits you to choose from the list of possible decision alternatives.

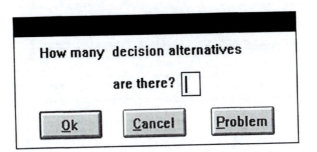

The line to A represents which decision alternative?

- develop prototype
- do not develop
- successful development (XYZ buys)
- unsuccessful development
- manual assembly

Ok    Problem    Cancel

Select the correct initial decision alternatives. Again, you have the option to **Cancel** or to view the **Problem**. If you cancel, you will return to the beginning of the problem. To select an alternative, highlight the alternative and select **Ok**. Continue selecting alternatives for each branch.

After the initial decision alternatives are selected, you are given an opportunity to change any decisions that you have made.

If you select **Yes**, you will return to the beginning of the problem.

If you select **No**, you will be told if your answer is correct or incorrect.

If your answer is incorrect, the following box will appear on the screen.

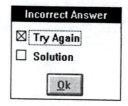

Select **Try Again** to return to the beginning of the problem or select **Solution** to receive the correct solution.

If you are incorrect twice, you will be given the solution.

## SECTION 2

Now that you have completed the initial decision branch, you need to formulate the branches emerging from the initial branches.

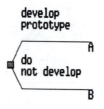

Click on the red letter with your mouse.

Branches can either be composed of decision alternatives, states of nature, or be the end of a path.

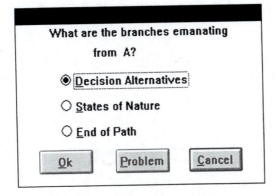

Selecting **End of Path** signals that the particular branch is complete.

When **Decision Alternatives** or **States of Nature** are selected, you must decide how many branches are emanating from the previous branch and select an alternative for each branch.

If **States of Nature** is selected, the probability associated with each state of nature must be entered. The probability must be a number between 0 and 1.

After completing a branch, you will be asked if you would like to make any changes.

If you select **Y**es, you will go back to the last decision.

If you select**N**o, you will be told whether your answer is correct or incorrect.

Repeat **Section 2** until all branches result in an **End of Path**.

## Certification Mode

Go to the main menu and select **Certification**.

To acquire certification, you must diagram 50 nodes without accumulating more than 4 strikes. A strike is given for each error made.

# Decision Tree Solving

This tutorial is designed to develop skills in the determination of the payoffs, expected values, and decisions involved in solving decision trees. A decision tree is a graphical depiction of the alternatives available to a decision maker and the possible outcome of each alternative.

## To Begin

Select **Help** from the main menu and read each of the topics.

## Practice Mode

Go to the main menu and select **Practice**.

### Viewing the Problem

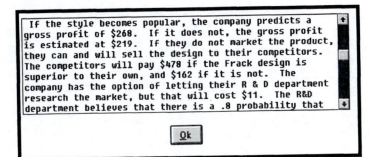

You may need to scroll to view the entire problem. While viewing the problem, you should take notes on the parameters of the problem.

Select **Ok** to continue.

You will want to view the problem from time to time. To do so, select **Problem**.

## Quitting the Problem

If you wish to leave the problem, select the **Quit** button.

**Caution:** If you leave the problem, all of your work will be lost.

## STAGE 1     Determining the Payoffs

The first portion of the tutorial requires you to determine the monetary payoffs at each endpoint of the decision tree.

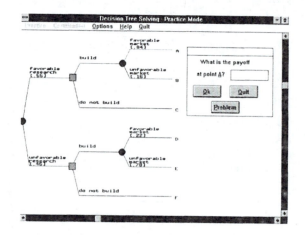

Once you determine the payoff at a particular endpoint, enter the solution in the box and select **Ok**.

If your answer is incorrect, the following box will appear on the screen:

Select **Try Again** to return to the beginning of the problem, or select **Solution** to receive the correct solution.

37

If you are incorrect twice, you will be given the solution.

Repeat **STAGE 1** until the payoff has been determined for each of the endpoints.

## STAGE 2    Determining the Expected Value of a Decision

In the second portion of the tutorial, you are asked to determine the expected value for the decision alternatives and to decide which decision is the best choice.

### Part 1    Determining Expected Values

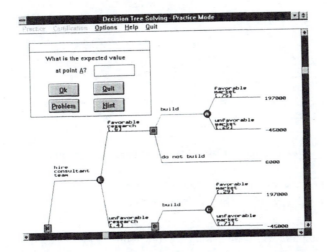

Once you have determined the expected value of a particular branch cluster, enter that value in the box and select **Ok**.

If you need help to answer the question, select **Hint**.

If your answer is incorrect, you may either **Try Again** or view the correct **Solution**.

If you are incorrect twice, you will be given the correct solution.

## Part 2      **Determining the Best Decision**

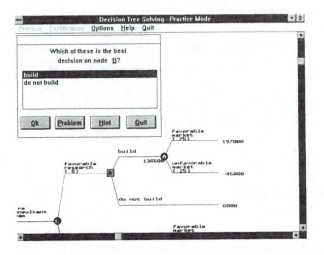

Once you have determined the best decision, highlight your answer and select **O**k.

If you need help to answer the question, select **H**int.

If your answer is incorrect, you may either **T**ry **Again**,or view the correct **S**olution.

If you are incorrect twice, you will be given the correct solution.

Repeat **STAGE 2** until the tree is complete.

# Certification Mode

Go to the main menu and select **C**ertification.

To acquire certification, you must solve 2 problems without accumulating more than 4 strikes. A strike is given for each error made.

# Forecasting Methods

This program provides tutorial exercises to develop experience in working with forecasting concepts. The program provides problems for four forecasting methods:

1. Linear Trend
2. Moving Average
3. Naive
4. Single Exponential Smoothing

## The Method Option

The **Method** option only applies to the Practice Mode. You may either answer questions on one forecasting method or on a combination of all four methods.

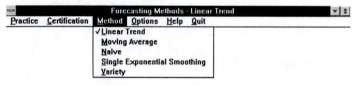

<u>Selecting a Method</u>

1. Go to the main menu and select **Method**.

2. When the pull-down menu appears, select the forecasting method that you wish to practice or select **Variety** to practice all four methods.

## To Begin

Select **Help** from the main menu and read each of the topics.

## Practice Mode

Go to the main menu and select **Practice**.

**Step 1** (only for the Linear Trend method)

Read the problem and decide which variable is the dependent variable. (You will need to scroll to view the entire problem.)

If you need help, select **Hint**. After the hint is shown, **Hint** will be disabled.

If you wish to go back to the main menu, select **Cancel**.

**Caution:** If you select **Cancel**, you will lose all previous work.

```
┌─────────────────────────────────────────────────┐
│ ┌─────────────────────────────────────────────┐ │
│ │   Given the number of strikes that occurred in the ▲│ │
│ │ U.S. in previous years, estimate the number of  │ │
│ │ strikes in the next year using the linear trend │ │
│ │ method.                                         │ │
│ │   Here are the previous years' numbers:        │ │
│ │                                                 │ │
│ │      Year        Number of Strikes             │ │
│ │      ───         ─────────────────             │ │
│ │       1               392                    ▼│ │
│ └─────────────────────────────────────────────┘ │
│          Which is the dependent variable?        │
│   ◉ 1 - the year                                 │
│   ○ 2 - the number of strikes that occurred      │
│   ┌─────────┐   ┌─────────┐   ┌─────────┐        │
│   │   Ok    │   │  Hint   │   │ Cancel  │        │
│   └─────────┘   └─────────┘   └─────────┘        │
│        ┌─────────────┐  ┌─────────────┐          │
│        │ Calculator  │  │    Help     │          │
│        └─────────────┘  └─────────────┘          │
└─────────────────────────────────────────────────┘
```

Make a selection and then select **Ok**.

If your answer is incorrect, you will be given the correct solution.

## Step 2 (only for the Linear Trend method)

The values for the slope and y-intercept are shown. You might want to write them down. Select **Ok** to continue.

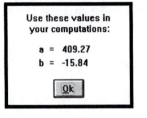

Use these values in
your computations:

a  =  409.27
b  =  -15.84

Ok

## Step 3 (all methods)

Given the number of strikes that occurred in the
U.S. in previous years, estimate the number of
strikes in the next year using the linear trend
method.
   Here are the previous years' numbers:

| Year | Number of Strikes |
|------|-------------------|
| 1    | 392               |

Enter Forecast:

| Ok | Hint | Graph | Regress |
|----|------|-------|---------|
| Cancel | Help | | Calculator |

## The Hint Option

The first time that you select **Hint**, the program provides the general formula for the forecast method.

The second time that you select **Hint**, the program provides the formula for the forecast method after the parameters given in the problem have been substituted.

The third time that you select **Hint**, the program provides the solution.

42

## The Graph Option

The **Graph** option gives you a graph showing the actual data and the forecasted value. If you are using the Linear Trend method, the graph also shows the regression function.

### The Regress Option (only for the Linear Trend method)

The **Regress** option gives you values for the slope and y-intercept to use in your computations.

### The Cancel Option

The **Cancel** option enables you to return to the main menu at any time. **Caution:** If you select **Cancel**, you will lose all previous work.

### Solving the Problem

Read the problem. (If you selected **Variety** from the **Method** pull-down menu, you will need to determine the forecasting method.) Compute the forecasted value for the next period, enter the value into the box provided, and then select **Ok**.

If your answer is incorrect, the correct answer will be provided for you.

# Certification Mode

Go to the main menu and select **Certification**.

In the Certification Mode you will be answering questions on a combination of all four methods. To acquire certification, you must complete 2 sets of 4 forecasting problems without accumulating more than 2 strikes. A strike is given for each error made.

# Reliability & Redundancy

Level A
Find system reliability for a system in series with no backups.
Level B
Find system reliability for a system in series with backups.
Level C
Draw a system in series and then find system reliability.

## Step 1          Demonstration Mode

Select **Demonstration** from the main menu.

The Demonstration Mode gives you step by step instructions on how to use the Reliability & Redundancy module.

To see the next page, select **Next Step** .

To see the previous page, select **Prior Step**.

When you are ready to begin practicing, select **End Demo** to end the Demonstration Mode.

## Step 2          Practice Mode

Select **Practice** from the main menu.

Continue solving problems in the Practice Mode until you feel that you have mastered the topic and are ready to certify.

## Step 3          Certification Mode

Select **Certification** from the main menu.

To acquire certification, you must complete 5 problems, consisting of 4 or 5 steps each, without accumulating more than 2 strikes.  A strike is given for each error made.

# Reliability: Normal Failure Times

In this module, you are given information about the service life of a product and are asked three different questions about the product. The questions are asked in "Steps". There will be two questions regarding the probability that the product will survive for a certain period of time and one question regarding the product life. The service lives are assumed to have a normal distribution.

**Step 1**      **Demonstration Mode**

Select **D**emonstration from the main menu.

The Demonstration Mode gives you step by step instructions on how to use the Reliability: Normal Failure Times module.

To see the next page select **N**ext Step .

To see the previous page, select **P**rior Step.

When you are ready to begin practicing, select **E**nd Demo to end the Demonstration Mode.

**Step 2**      **Practice Mode**

Select**P**ractice from the main menu. Continue solving problems in the Practice Mode until you feel that you have mastered the topic and are ready to certify.

**Step 3**      **Certification Mode**

Select **C**ertification from the main menu.

To acquire certification, you must complete 6 problems, consisting of 3 steps each, without accumulating more than 2 strikes. A strike is given for each error made.

# Reliability: Exponential Failure Times

In this module, you are given information about the service life of a product and are asked three different questions about the product. The questions are asked in "Steps". There will be two questions regarding the probability that the product will survive for a certain period of time and one question regarding the product life. The service lives are assumed to have an exponential distribution.

### Step 1          Demonstration Mode

Select **Demonstration** from the main menu.

The Demonstration Mode gives you step by step instructions on how to use the Reliability: Exponential Failure Times module.

To see the next page select **Next Step** .

To see the previous page, select **Prior Step**.

When you are ready to begin practicing, select **End Demo** to end the Demonstration Mode.

### Step 2          Practice Mode

Select **Practice** from the main menu. Continue solving problems in the Practice Mode until you feel that you have mastered the topic and are ready to certify.

### Step 3          Certification Mode

Select **Certification** from the main menu.

To acquire certification, you must complete 6 problems, consisting of 3 steps each, without accumulating more than 2 strikes. A strike is given for each error made.

# Linear Programming I & II

These modules provide tutorial exercises to help develop skills in the formulation of linear programming problems. In the formulation exercises, you will identify decision variables, develop the objective function, and formulate the constraints.

## To Begin

Select **Help** from the main menu and read each of the topics.

## Practice Mode

Go to the main menu and select **Practice**.

### Step 1          Viewing the Problem

The box at the top of the screen contains the problem. You might need to scroll to view the entire problem.

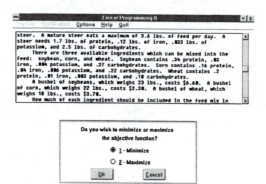

## Step 2     Collecting Pertinent Information

Carefully read the problem. Then, identify the decision variables, the objective function, and the constraints. We suggest that you record these values on paper.

## Step 3     Formulating the Problem

### PHASE I

The first portion of the tutorial requires you to determine whether the goal of the objective function is to minimize cost or to maximize profit or revenues.

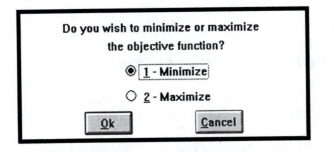

Make a selection by using the mouse or by pressing one of the underlined numbers.

If you are incorrect, you will be given the correct answer.

## PHASE II

The second phase of the tutorial requires you to determine the decision variables of the problem. Select the decision variables from the list provided for you.

| Select a Decision Variable |
| --- |
| Select a variable from the following list: |

```
the carbohydrate content of corn                          ↑
the cost of a pound of corn
the cost of a pound of wheat
the carbohydrate content of wheat
the daily carbohydrate requirement of a steer
the cost of a pound of soybean                            ↓
```

[ Ok ]     [ Finished ]     [ Cancel ]

Make a selection by highlighting your choice with the blue bar. You can select the variable that you want by using your mouse or by manipulating the blue bar with the arrow keys. When you have made your selection, select **Ok**.

If the variable that you selected is not a decision variable, the following dialog box will appear:

```
Your answer is not correct.

Your Selection:

the cost of a pound of corn

is a coefficient of the

objective function.

[ Ok ]
```

In this example, the selected variable is a coefficient of the objective function rather than a decision variable.

Select **Ok** to continue.

If the variable you select is a decision variable of the problem, the following dialog box will appear:

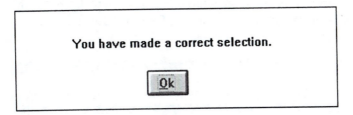

**You have made a correct selection.**

[Ok]

Select **Ok** to continue.

Continue to select decision variables until you believe that you have selected all of the variables of the problem. Then, record your decision by selecting **Finished**.

If you did not select all of the variables, the program will list the variables that you omitted.

---

**Select a Decision Variable**

These variables were not selected:

the number of one-sided, four-color pages to print
the number of double-sided, one-color pages to print
the number of one-sided, one-color pages to print

[Ok]    [Finished]    [Cancel]

---

Select **Ok** to continue.

After selecting the decision variables, symbolic identifiers are attached.

---

The symbols used for the decision variables are given below:

p = acres of red clay planted with wheat
q = acres of red clay planted with corn
r = acres of sandy loam planted with wheat
s = acres of sandy loam planted with corn
t = acres of sandy loam planted with cotton

[Ok]

---

50

The variable names, **p**, **q**, **r**, **s**, and **t** in the example given, are used to formulate the objective function and the constraints.

Select **Ok** to continue.

## PHASE III

The next portion of the tutorial requires you to determine the objective function and the constraints of the problem.

When determining the objective function and the constraints, six options will be available to you.

1. **Submit**    Press <Enter> or select **Submit** to submit the objective function or constraint that you have just completed.

2. **Hint**    The first time that you select **Hint**, the program provides questions that will help you to develop the objective function and the constraints. The second time you select **Hint**, the program provides the solution.

51

3. **Constraints**   Select **Constraint** to list the constraints that you have submitted.

4. **Variables**   Select **Variables** to view the list of decision variables and their symbols.

5. **Finished**   Select **Finished** when you have entered all of the constraints.

6. **Quit**   Press <Esc> or select the **Quit** button to leave the problem.

## Formulating the Objective Function

The objective function is not a statement of equality or inequality. To formulate the objective function, determine the amount that one unit of each variable contributes to the profit or cost. This amount is the coefficient of that variable.

```
Enter the Objective Function:

73.75p + 75.6q + 64.9r + 68.4s + 92.4t

        <F1>: ≤     <F2>: ≥     <F3>: ≠

      Submit            Hint            Finished

      Constraints       Variables       Quit
```

Select **Submit** to enter the objective function.

## Selecting a Resource Constraint

```
                    Select a Constraint

          Which constraint do you wish to enter?

 one-sided, one-color page minimum production constraint      ▲
 double-sided, one-color page minimum production constraint
 one-sided, four-color page minimum production constraint
 one-sided, one-color page maximum production constraint      ▼

                    ┌─────────────┐
                    │     Ok      │
                    └─────────────┘
```

Select a constraint and then select **Ok** to continue.

## Formulating a Resource Constraint

To formulate a resource constraint, determine the amount of the resource in each variable and the amount of the resource available.

```
 Enter the red clay resource constraint:

 p + q ≤ 36|

              <F1>: ≤     <F2>: ≥     <F3>: ≠

      Submit            Hint            Finished

      Constraints       Variables       Quit
```

Select **Submit** to enter the resource constraint.

**Special keys used in formulating constraints:**

F1  ≤
F2  ≥
F3  ≠

When you believe that all the constraints have been entered, select **Finished**.

If you did not determine all of the problem's constraints, the ones that you omitted will be listed. If you correctly formulated all of the constraints, the problem will end and you will return to the main menu.

Select **Practice** to work another problem.

# Certification Mode

Go to the main menu and select **Certification**.

To acquire certification, you must complete 3 Linear Programming problems without accumulating more than 4 strikes. A strike is given for each formulation error made.

# Line Balancing

In this module, you are asked to develop a graphical represen-
tation of production activities and then balance the line using
the criteria in the problem.

**Step 1**      **Demonstration Mode**

Select **Demonstration** from the main menu.

The Demonstration Mode gives you step by step instructions on
how to use the Line Balancing module.

To see the next page, select **Next Step**.

To see the previous page, select **Prior Step**.

When you are ready to begin practicing, select **End Demo** to
end the Demonstration Mode.

**Step 2**      **Practice Mode**

Select **Practice** from the main menu.

Continue solving problems in the Practice Mode until you feel
that you have mastered the topic and are ready to certify.

**Step 3**      **Certification Mode**

Select **Certification** from the main menu.

To acquire certification, you must complete 5 problems,
consisting of 7 steps each, without accumulating more than 4
strikes. A strike is given for each error made.

# Learning Curves

In this module, you are given a word problem containing parameters related to the learning curve model and asked to solve for either the learning curve percentage, the time to complete the first unit, the total time required to complete a certain number of units, or the time to complete the $n^{th}$ unit.

## Step 1      Demonstration Mode

Select **Demonstration** from the main menu.

The Demonstration Mode gives you step by step instructions on how to use the Learning Curves module.

To see the next page, select **Next Step**.

To see the previous page, select **Prior Step**.

When you are ready to begin practicing, select **End Demo** to end the Demonstration Mode.

## Step 2      Practice Mode

Select **Practice** from the main menu.

Continue solving problems in the Practice Mode until you feel that you have mastered the topic and are ready to certify.

## Step 3      Certification Mode

Select **Certification** from the main menu.

To acquire certification, you must complete 10 problems, without accumulating more than 2 strikes. A strike is given for each error made.

# Mean Charts: Using the Range

In this module, you are given the results of sampling from a process and are asked to construct and interpret a mean chart which uses the sample range to measure process variation. Each problem consists of 5 steps.

### Step 1 — Demonstration Mode

Select **Demonstration** from the main menu.

The Demonstration Mode gives you step by step instructions on how to use the Mean Charts: Using the Range module.

To see the next page, select **Next Step**.

To see the previous page, select **Prior Step**.

When you are ready to begin practicing, select **End Demo** to end the Demonstration Mode.

### Step 2 — Practice Mode

Select **Practice** from the main menu.

Continue solving problems in the Practice Mode until you feel that you have mastered the topic and are ready to certify.

### Step 3 — Certification Mode

Select **Certification** from the main menu.

To acquire certification, you must complete 5 problems, consisting of 5 steps each, without accumulating more than 3 strikes. A strike is given for each error made.

# Mean Charts: Using s

In this module, you are given the results of sampling from a process and are asked to construct and interpret a mean chart which uses the sample standard deviation to estimate process variation. Each problem consists of 5 steps.

## Step 1          Demonstration Mode

Select **Demonstration** from the main menu.

The Demonstration Mode gives you step by step instructions on how to use the Mean Charts: Using s module.

To see the next page select **Next Step**.

To see the previous page, select **Prior Step**.

When you are ready to begin practicing, select **End Demo** to end the Demonstration Mode.

## Step 2          Practice Mode

Select **Practice** from the main menu.

Continue solving problems in the Practice Mode until you feel that you have mastered the topic and are ready to certify.

## Step 3          Certification Mode

Select **Certification** from the main menu.

To acquire certification, you must complete 5 problems, consisting of 5 steps each, without accumulating more than 3 strikes. A strike is given for each error made.

# R - Chart

In this module, you are given the results of sampling from a process and are asked to construct and interpret an R - Chart. Each problem consists of 5 steps.

### Step 1    Demonstration Mode

Select **Demonstration** from the main menu.

The Demonstration Mode gives you step by step instructions on how to use the R - Chart module.

To see the next page, select **Next Step**.

To see the previous page, select **Prior Step**.

When you are ready to begin practicing, select **End Demo** to end the Demonstration Mode.

### Step 2    Practice Mode

Select **Practice** from the main menu.

Continue solving problems in the Practice Mode until you feel that you have mastered the topic and are ready to certify.

### Step 3    Certification Mode

Select **Certification** from the main menu.

To acquire certification, you must complete 5 problems, consisting of 5 steps each, without accumulating more than 3 strikes. A strike is given for each error made.

# p - Chart

In this module, you are given the results of sampling from a process and are asked to construct and interpret a p - Chart. Each problem consists of 5 steps.

### Step 1          Demonstration Mode

Select **Demonstration** from the main menu.

The Demonstration Mode gives you step by step instructions on how to use the p - Chart module.

To see the next page, select **Next Step**.

To see the previous page, select **Prior Step**.

When you are ready to begin practicing, select **End Demo** to end the Demonstration Mode.

### Step 2          Practice Mode

Select **Practice** from the main menu.

Continue solving problems in the Practice Mode until you feel that you have mastered the topic and are ready to certify.

### Step 3          Certification Mode

Select **Certification** from the main menu.

To acquire certification, you must complete 5 problems, consisting of 5 steps each, without accumulating more than 3 strikes. A strike is given for each error made.

# c - Chart

In this module, you are given the results of sampling from a process and are asked to construct and interpret a c - Chart. Each problem consists of 5 steps.

### Step 1        Demonstration Mode

Select **Demonstration** from the main menu.

The Demonstration Mode gives you step by step instructions on how to use the c - Chart module.

To see the next page, select **Next Step**.

To see the previous page, select **Prior Step**.

When you are ready to begin practicing, select **End Demo** to end the Demonstration Mode.

### Step 2        Practice Mode

Select **Practice** from the main menu.

Continue solving problems in the Practice Mode until you feel that you have mastered the topic and are ready to certify.

### Step 3        Certification Mode

Select **Certification** from the main menu.

To acquire certification, you must complete 5 problems, consisting of 5 steps each, without accumulating more than 3 strikes. A strike is given for each error made.

# Inventory Word Problems

This program provides tutorial exercises to develop experience in working with inventory models. Two inventory models are used in this tutorial.

1. The Economic Order Quantity (EOQ) Model

2. The Quantity Discount Model

## To Begin

Select **Help** from the main menu and read each of the topics.

## Practice Mode

Go to the main menu and select **Practice**.

### Determination of the Model

Read the problem and determine the appropriate model.

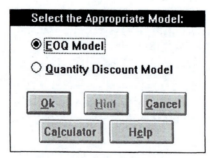

Select **EOQ Model** or **Quantity Discount Model**, and then select **Ok**.

The tutorial will tell you if your response is correct or incorrect.

61

# The Economic Order Quantity Model

If the model given in the problem was an **EOQ Model,** use this section. Otherwise, go to the section titled The Quantity Discount Model.

The purpose of the EOQ Model is to identify the optimal order quantity so that the cost associated with inventory can be minimized. There are 5 steps in the solution of the EOQ Model problem. The dialog boxes will prompt you for an answer in each step. The tutorial will tell you if your response is correct or incorrect after each answer.

## The Hint Option

The first time that you select **Hint**, the program provides the formula of the function under consideration.

The second time that you select **Hint**, the program provides the variables needed to compute the function under consideration.

The third time that you select **Hint**, the program provides the complete solution.

## Quitting the Problem

If you wish to leave the problem, select **Cancel**.

**Caution**: If you leave the problem, you will return to the main menu and all of your previous work will be lost.

**Step 1**

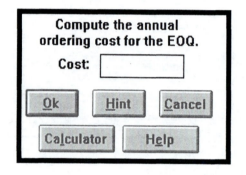

**Step 2**

**Step 3**

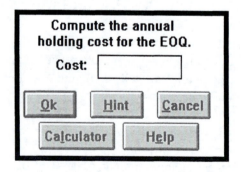

**Step 4**

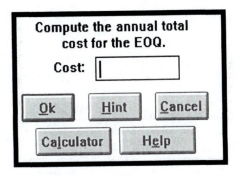

**Step 5**

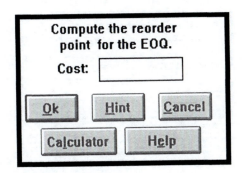

You have completed the problem.

# The Quantity Discount Model

There are 8 steps in the solution of the Quantity Discount Model problem. The dialog boxes will prompt you for an answer in each step. The tutorial will tell you if your response is correct or incorrect after each answer.

### The Hint Option

For **Step 1** there is only one hint. The **Hint** button will be disabled after the hint is shown.

For **Step 2 - Step 8** :

The first time that you select **Hint**, the program provides the formula of the function under consideration,

The second time that you select **Hint**, the program provides the variables needed to compute the function under consideration,

The third time that you select **Hint**, the program provides the complete solution.

## Quitting the Problem

If you wish to leave the problem, select **Cancel**.

**Caution**: If you leave the problem, all of your work will be lost.

## Step 1

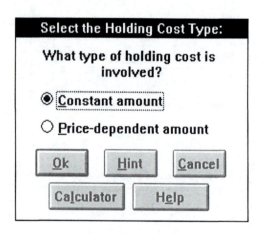

## Step 2

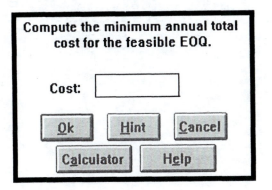

**At what price is the EOQ feasible?**

Price: $ [        ]

[Ok] [Hint] [Cancel]
[Calculator] [Help]

**Step 3** (This step will be skipped under the constant holding cost model.)

**Find the feasible EOQ.**

EOQ: [        ]

[Ok] [Hint] [Cancel]
[Calculator] [Help]

## Step 4

**Compute the minimum annual total cost for the feasible EOQ.**

Cost: [        ]

[Ok] [Hint] [Cancel]
[Calculator] [Help]

## Step 5 - Step 7

Compute the minimum annual total cost in the increments
stated.  The following box is an example.

```
┌─────────────────────────────────┐
│  Compute the minimum annual     │
│  total cost for orders of 120 to│
│            239 units.           │
│                                 │
│     Cost:  [              ]     │
│                                 │
│  [ Ok ]   [ Hint ]   [ Cancel ] │
│    [ Calculator ]   [ Help ]    │
└─────────────────────────────────┘
```

## Step 8

```
┌─────────────────────────────────┐
│ How many units should be ordered│
│    to minimize the total cost?  │
│                                 │
│     Units: [              ]     │
│                                 │
│  [ Ok ]   [ Hint ]   [ Cancel ] │
│    [ Calculator ]   [ Help ]    │
└─────────────────────────────────┘
```

You have completed the problem.

# Certification Mode

Go to the main menu and select **Certification**.

To acquire certification, you must complete 6 inventory
problems without accumulating more than 5 strikes. A strike
is given for each error made.

# Material Requirements Planning

This module requires you to level code the given product tree, fill a bill of materials, fill a master schedule and develop the material requirements plan for a particular component.

### Step 1     Demonstration Mode

Select **Demonstration** from the main menu.

The Demonstration Mode gives you step by step instructions on how to use the Material Requirements Planning module.

To see the next page, select **Next Step** .

To see the previous page, select **Prior Step**.

When you are ready to begin practicing, select **End Demo** to end the Demonstration Mode.

### Step 2     Practice Mode

Select **Practice** from the main menu.

Continue solving problems in the Practice Mode until you feel that you have mastered the topic and are ready to certify.

### Step 3     Certification Mode

Select **Certification** from the main menu.

To acquire certification, you must complete 5 problems, consisting of 4 steps each, without accumulating more than 4 strikes. A strike is given for each error made.

# CPM I

In this module, you are given a list of activities, expected times, and precedence relationships, and are asked to:
- draw an on-arc precedence diagram,
- choose activities on the critical path, and
- determine the length of the critical path.

## Step 1      Demonstration Mode

Select **Demonstration** from the main menu.

The Demonstration Mode gives you step by step instructions on how to use the CPM I module.

To see the next page, select **Next Step**.

To see the previous page, select **Prior Step**.

When you are ready to begin practicing, select **End Demo** to end the Demonstration Mode.

## Step 2      Practice Mode

Select **Practice** from the main menu.

Continue solving problems in the Practice Mode until you feel that you have mastered the topic and are ready to certify.

## Step 3      Certification Mode

Select **Certification** from the main menu.

To acquire certification, you must complete 5 problems, consisting of 3 steps each, without accumulating more than 3 strikes. A strike is given for each error made.

# CPM II

In this module, you are given an on-arc network diagram and are asked to:

- find the critical path,
- determine the expected length of the project,
- calculate ES, EF, LS, and LF for each activity, and
- calculate slack time for each activity.

**Step 1**      **Demonstration Mode**

Select **Demonstration** from the main menu.

The Demonstration Mode gives you step by step instructions on how to use the CPM II module.

To see the next page, select **Next Step** .

To see the previous page, select **Prior Step**.

When you are ready to begin practicing, select **End Demo** to end the Demonstration Mode.

**Step 2**      **Practice Mode**

Select **Practice** from the main menu.

Continue solving problems in the Practice Mode until you feel that you have mastered the topic and are ready to certify.

**Step 3**      **Certification Mode**

Select **Certification** from the main menu.

To acquire certification, you must complete 3 problems, consisting of 5 steps each, without accumulating more than 2 strikes. A strike is given for each error made.

# PERT

In this module, you are given a list of activities, expected times, and precedence relationships, and are asked to draw an on-arc precedence diagram, find the expected time for each activity, find the variance of each activity, identify the paths, expected time, and standard deviation for each path, identify the critical path, and find the probability of completion of the project by N weeks (N < length of critical path).

## Step 1          Demonstration Mode

Select **Demonstration** from the main menu.

The Demonstration Mode gives you step by step instructions on how to use the PERT module.

To see the next page, select **Next Step** .

To see the previous page, select **Prior Step**.

When you are ready to begin practicing, select **End Demo** to end the Demonstration Mode.

## Step 2          Practice Mode

Select **Practice** from the main menu. Continue solving problems in the Practice Mode until you feel that you have mastered the topic and are ready to certify.

## Step 3          Certification Mode

Select **Certification** from the main menu.

To acquire certification, you must complete 3 problems, consisting of 6 steps each, without accumulating more than 2 strikes. A strike is given for each error made.

71

# Queuing Problems

These tutorial exercises develop experience in working with queuing concepts. The objective of queuing theory is to analyze the amount of time a unit spends in the system. Three models are used in this tutorial.

1. The Single-Channel Model
2. The Multiple-Channel Model
3. The Constant Service Time Model

## To Begin

Select **Help** from the main menu and read each of the topics.

## Practice Mode

Go to the main menu and select **Practice**.

### Determination of the Model

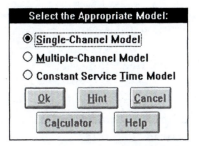

Read the problem and determine the appropriate model.

If you need help answering the question, select **Hint**. After **Hint** is selected once, it will be disabled.

Select **Single-Channel Model**, **Multiple-Channel Model**, or **Constant Service Time Model**, and then select **Ok**.

# The Single-Channel Model

There are 9 steps in the solution of the Single-Channel Model problem. The dialog boxes will prompt you for an answer in each step. The tutorial will tell you if your response is correct or incorrect after each answer.

## The Hint Option

For **Step 1** and **Step 2** there is only one hint. The **Hint** button will be disabled after the hint is shown.

For **Step 3** - **Step 9** :

The first time that you select **Hint**, the program provides the formula of the function under consideration,

The second time that you select **Hint**, the program provides the variables needed to compute the function under consideration,

The third time that you select **Hint**, the program provides the solution.

## Quitting the Problem

If you wish to leave the problem, select **Cancel**.

**Caution**: If you leave the problem, all of your work will be lost.

## Step 1

Determine the average arrival rate based on the problem parameters and enter it in the dialog box below.

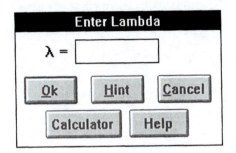

## Step 2

Determine the average service rate.

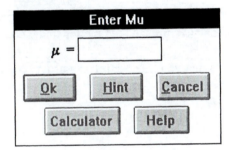

### Step 3

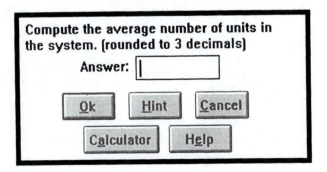

## Step 4

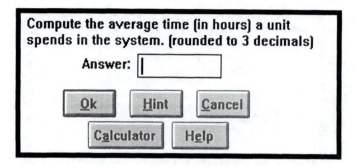

## Step 5

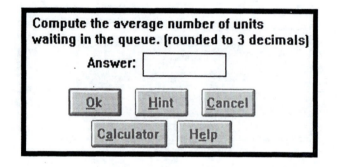

## Step 6

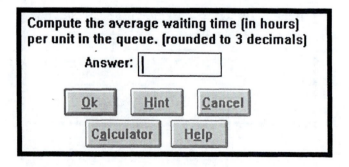

## Step 7

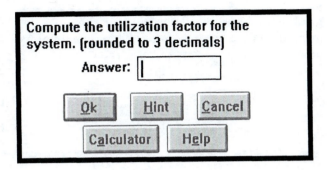

## Step 8

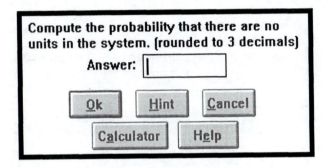

## Step 9

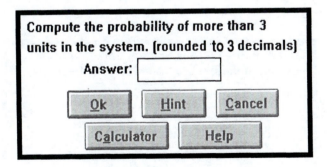

You have completed the problem.

# The Multiple-Channel Model

There are 8 steps in the solution of the Multiple-Channel Model problem. The dialog boxes will prompt you for an answer in each step. The tutorial will tell you if your response is correct or incorrect after each answer.

## The Hint Option

For **Step 1** - **Step 3** there is only one hint. The **Hint** button will be disabled after the hint is shown.

For **Step 4** - **Step 8** :

The first time that you select **Hint**, the program provides the formula of the function under consideration,

The second time that you select **Hint**, the program provides the variables needed to compute the function under consideration,

The third time that you select **Hint**, the program provides the solution.

## Quitting the Problem

If you wish to leave the problem, select **Cancel**.

**Caution**: If you leave the problem, all of your work will be lost.

## Step 1

Determine the average arrival rate based on the problem parameters and enter it in the dialog box.

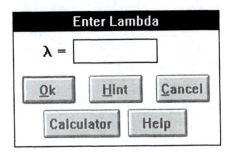

## Step 2

Determine the average service rate.

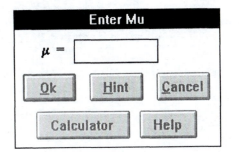

## Step 3

Compute the maximum number of channels.

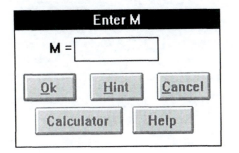

## Step 4

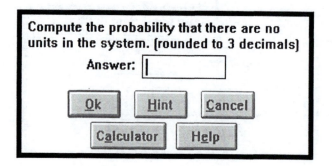

Compute the probability that there are no units in the system. (rounded to 3 decimals)

Answer: [ ]

[ Ok ]  [ Hint ]  [ Cancel ]

[ Calculator ]  [ Help ]

## Step 5

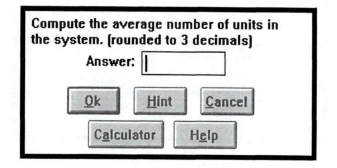

Compute the average number of units in the system. (rounded to 3 decimals)

Answer: [ ]

[ Ok ]  [ Hint ]  [ Cancel ]

[ Calculator ]  [ Help ]

## Step 6

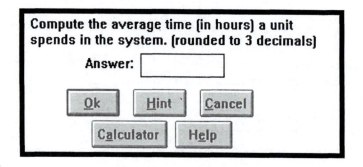

Compute the average time (in hours) a unit spends in the system. (rounded to 3 decimals)

Answer: [ ]

[ Ok ]  [ Hint ]  [ Cancel ]

[ Calculator ]  [ Help ]

## Step 7

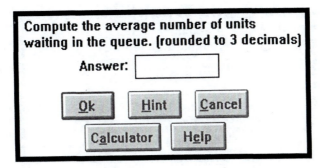

## Step 8

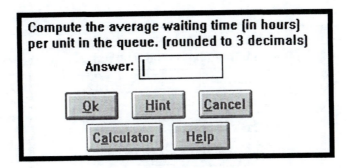

You have completed the problem.

# The Constant Service Time Model

There are 6 steps in the solution of the Constant Service Time Model problem. The dialog boxes will prompt you for an answer in each step. The tutorial will tell you if your response is correct or incorrect after each answer.

## The Hint Option

For **Step 1** and **Step 2** there is only one hint. The **Hint** button will be disabled after the hint is shown.

For **Step 3** - **Step 6** :

The first time that you select **Hint**, the program provides the formula of the function under consideration,

The second time that you select **Hint**, the program provides the variables needed to compute the function under consideration,

The third time that you select **Hint**, the program provides the solution.

## Quitting the Problem

If you wish to leave the problem, select **Cancel**.

**Caution**: If you leave the problem, all of your work will be lost.

## Step 1

Determine the average arrival rate based on the problem parameters and enter it in the dialog box.

Enter Lambda

$\lambda =$ [ ]

| Ok | Hint | Cancel |

| Calculator | Help |

## Step 2

Determine the average service rate.

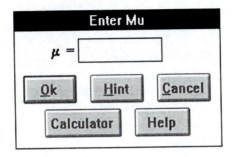

## Step 3

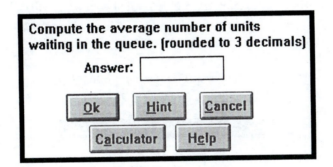

## Step 4

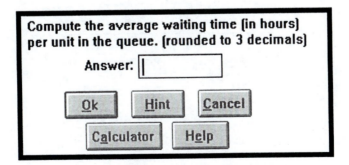

## Step 5

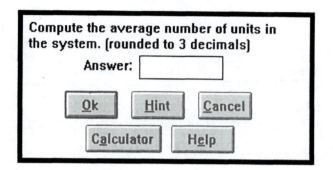

## Step 6

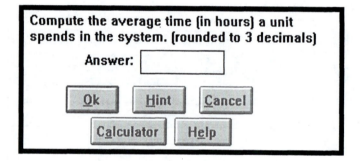

You have completed the problem.

# Certification Mode

Go to the main menu and select **Certification**.

To acquire certification, you must complete 5 queuing problems without accumulating more than 4 strikes. A strike is given for each error made.

# Record Book

|  | Due Date | Certification # |
|---|---|---|
| Decision Tree Building |  |  |
| Decision Tree Solving |  |  |
| Forecasting Methods |  |  |
| Reliability & Redundancy |  |  |
| Reliability: Normal Failure Times |  |  |
| Reliability: Exponential Failure Times |  |  |
| Linear Programming I |  |  |
| Linear Programming II |  |  |
| Line Balancing |  |  |
| Learning Curves |  |  |
| Mean Charts: Using the Range |  |  |
| Mean Charts: Using s |  |  |
| R - Chart |  |  |
| p - Chart |  |  |
| c - Chart |  |  |
| Inventory Word Problems |  |  |
| Material Requirements Planning |  |  |
| CPM I |  |  |
| CPM II |  |  |
| PERT |  |  |
| Queuing Problems |  |  |

# ADVENTURES IN OPERATIONS MANAGEMENT

**BY OPENING THIS PACKAGE YOU HAVE ACCEPTED THE LICENSE AGREEMENT BELOW.**

## LICENSE AGREEMENT

ISBN 0-918091-09-8

08-AAV-567